GENESIS

Because of HIS great love, He made a world and called it Earth
His love is evident in all of creation, every detail big and small
From the lilies in the valley to the treetops of the mighty oak
In every creeping thing, and those that soar with wings
And it was because of this same LOVE that God made me

Book Cover & Illustrations by Nakisha Jackson

CONTENTS

Forward

Our attention is constantly battling and competing with the loud distractions in the world around us. The beeping and tweeting of notifications from social media, text messages, emails, phone calls, and appointments keep us on constant alert. The tugging of household chores, world news, mountainous challenges, taunting whispers that bribe us with sweet leftovers lurking in the fridge, and those nagging negative thoughts. Meditation, fasting, praying, and retreating are methods we use to press the mute button or simply lower the volume on life. When our hearts fight to comprehend and speak words that lay muffled beneath the ever-rising noises in our heads, we write. Whether it's in the form of journaling, poetry, song, a prayer, or a simple letter, spend time writing those unspoken thoughts. They may one day come to light, leading the way to our truth and the inner peace we seek.

Soul Searcher is a collection of original, heartfelt poetry that provokes our innermost thoughts to explore secret passions, high hopes and the deepest desires of the heart. Poems that reflect on visions and dreams freeing the imagination to sore beyond the limitations of our own abilities, giving way to the limitless power of The Most High. So let us all be reminded to acknowledge our Creator, accepting all that we are, and all that we were created to be.

This book of poetry is dedicated to my parents who are now with the Lord, for the gift of a strong foundation built on a love for God, God's Word, and God's people.

The Glory

I lift up my eyes to the mountains—where does my help come from? My help comes from the Lord, the Maker of heaven and earth. Psalm 121:1-2

The Maker

Morning arrived from a long-flighted journey
And for the very first time it was the break of dawn
Golden rays reached forth through the darkness
And stepped aside for a brand new sun
Unpretentiously and boldly it walked in and stood
Until the Creator saw that it was good
Across the earth spanned shoreless seas
There were no flowers, no shrubs, no trees
Just swirling waters beneath the atmosphere
But for The Maker --
The vision of heaven and earth was clear
Up through massive waters deep
Emerged dry land and mountains steep
Valleys they lay low and plants began to grow
Just because God said so!
Such immaculate power so perfect and profound
With His head in heaven and His feet on earth's ground
He took time out to make butterflies and bumblebees
And to cover the naked branches with leaves
Then in His perfect image, God made man
And a woman beside him, there she would stand
As they walked through the beautiful Garden of Eden
Where there satan first sought to deceive
Yes, he led us all astray... he led us all astray
But something happened one glorious day

When born in a little manger tucked away in the hay
Christ the Savior came to say...

I AM the Way, the Truth and the Life...

I AM the bread of life
I AM the LIGHT of the world
I AM the door - All that you're searching for
I AM the good shepherd
Holy Perfection - I AM the resurrection
Crucified for all mankind - I AM the vine
I AM... more than you can imagine
He's more than you can imagine
My God is more than you can imagine

The Metamorphism of the Butterfly

We praise God for the butterfly in all its magnificence and splendor. The Lord speaks to us through this small, living parable on patience and strength. As a mere egg unaware of the dangers in the world around it, it transformed from egg to caterpillar, from caterpillar to cocoon, and from cocoon to butterfly - God is there. Creeping and crawling along the ground, and from leaf to leaf among the trees, the caterpillar journeyed quite satisfied with what the Lord had done. For you see, there is a plentiful supply of leafy food to eat, and fresh morning dew to quench its thirst. So there the caterpillar nestled its full belly in a bed of shaded trees, and whispered "God's grace is sufficient for me." You see, even the caterpillar did praise the Lord!

Along this blissful journey, something began to happen. The caterpillar's cozy disposition is interrupted as its skin begins to decay and die. The caterpillar finds itself caught up in a change of life – called – the "Metamorphism of the Butterfly". Imagine that God has promised flight, beauty, and the world's adoration to this small, insignificant one who moves along its slithering belly to find its purpose in the world. Imagine that God says, do not be afraid, for I will never leave you. I will be with you from egg to caterpillar, from caterpillar to cocoon, from cocoon to butterfly, and even to the end of the world.

It is not an easy task for the creature, you see, to build a cocoon for the very first time. Other creatures of the grassy foliage consider the caterpillar strangely odd and peculiar. But, obediently the caterpillar toiled day after day – spinning a cocoon while struggling to escape its own dying flesh.

"I'll fly away. One grand morning, when this life is over, I will fly away." Wrapped in darkness and isolation the caterpillar encounters the season of the cocoon. A time to weep, a time to sleep – frozen in motion, emotions deep beneath its mossy cover – no longer free. But you see the cocoon is not a prison but protection; it is not isolation but a time of meditation and reflection. The cocoon is not a form of insect segregation, yet unification with the Creator of all creation – an education on restoration. There changing, maturing, trusting, and patiently waiting on the Lord. "No never alone, no never alone, Jesus promised never to leave me..."

The day of the awakening finally arrived. From the depths of the cocoon, emerged the butterfly. Reaching and stretching forth new legs, exposing brand new skin to the warm sun again. See its wings – beautiful artistry - hand-painted by God, bending open wide to catch a cool breeze as if for the very first time. Now taking flight beyond the cocoon and up through green trees, yellow daffodils, flowers in colors of purple and pink. Fluttering and swirling a holy dance of praise! I'm born again! I'm born again.

No Room

In a dying world filled with gloom
A sinful mankind was destined for doom
Then LOVE sat high and looked down low
And the Lamb of God said, "Send ME I'll go"

All the way from heaven to earth
The Bible tells of his virgin birth
God's Son – Miracle in a Manger
Turned away by neighbor and stranger
There was no golden crib
No fine linen bib
No servants with platters and silver spoons
No, for Mary's Baby they had no room

No room, no room
We live in a world that has no room
Prayer in our schools – no room
In our society today – no room
In our homes and relationships
For the Savior of the World we have no room

So there He was born in a stable
Oh worship Him now while you're able
So the shepherds left their flocks
Three wise men left their stocks
Bearing gifts, they did travel afar
Shown the way being led by a star
A star that shined brightly in the sky
To see the birth of the Son of the Most High

Each Christmas season
Day 25
Remember Love is the reason
That we are still alive
Now carry that love throughout the new year
Try to keep it going til Jesus reappears

Before the clutter of presents start
Make room for Christ in your heart
And let that room be fit for a King!
Let church bells ring
And angels sing
Glory – Glory to the New Born King!

Early Sunday Morning

Early Sunday morning came the dawning of a brand new day
Suddenly the earth trembled and the tombstone rolled away
An angel of the Lord came all the way from heaven down
And the guards filled with fear fell faintly to the ground
If you're looking for Jesus here among the dead
He is not here, for He has risen just as He said
Go now and tell them that our crucified Savior lives
The gift of Hope and Salvation to all He freely gives
Tell them of his crucifixion and of his resurrection
Some will follow Him; some will choose their own direction
Oh but tell them! Spread the Good News to everyone
That "God so loved the world that He gave His only Son
And whosoever believe in Him shall not perish
But shall have everlasting life." John 3:16

A Sunday Hallelujah

We sing holy, holy to his name
In the sanctuary we shout
Hallelujah, he reigns!
We tell the story of his virgin birth
And speak of his miracles here on earth
We open the doors with an invitation
For lost souls who seek salvation
We tell of all the sacrifices he made
Even unto the grave
where three days he stayed
We declare him as the risen Savior
on Sunday...

But who do you say Jesus is to you on Monday?

You said, God you are my everything
My healer, my strength, my KING
Yet when face to face with sin
Temptation wins again
Leaving God on the old church pews
Like old printed programs you can't use

On Sundays
we sing holy, holy to his name
in the sanctuary we shout
Hallelujah, he reigns!
We tell the story of his virgin birth
And speak of his miracles here on earth
We open the doors with an invitation
For lost souls who seek salvation
We tell of all the sacrifices he made
Even unto the grave
where three days he stayed
We declare him as the risen Savior
on Sunday...

But who do you say Jesus is to you
on Monday?

Remember Miracles

War and hatred all across the land
Lord take us back where we first began
The sweet peace of Eden's garden
Is reminiscent of life according
To Your will, and to Your plan
Let us find joy again
In the beauty of creation
And the vast illumination
Of the heavens—sun, moon and the bright morning star
For Your goodness we need not search far
But it's hard to forget all the heartache, and the pain
All the mistakes, the regrets, the tears and the shame
But when we look back on brighter days
We are reminded that trouble don't last always
Take us back Lord, to the remembrance of a past
When grandmothers and grandfathers of old
Let wisdom and truth be told

Whisper hymns in harmonious tones
That speak of a God that can raise dry bones
A Mighty God that did part the Red Sea
And forced old Pharaoh to set His children free
Remember a time when water turned to wine
And demons leaped from a man and entered into swine
Remember the 5000, didn't have enough food
God took 5 loaves, 2 fish and fed the multitude
Remember the giants and armies killed
Little girls, lepers, and blind men healed
Let us not forget that we were lost
Before our Savior paid the cost
Remember the Blood, remember the Cross
Remember Miracles

I See

When I rise up
and see the morning sun
I see the risen One
who died for me
with closed eyes
and an open heart
I climb the hill of calvary
to see a rugged cross
there it stands
Towering over me
I see the nails
I see the nails
Overwhelming horror
Chills my flesh
I see His heaving
Panting chest
Searching for breath
I hear him calling
Father!
Blood and water
Washes over me
I see his hung down head
For me

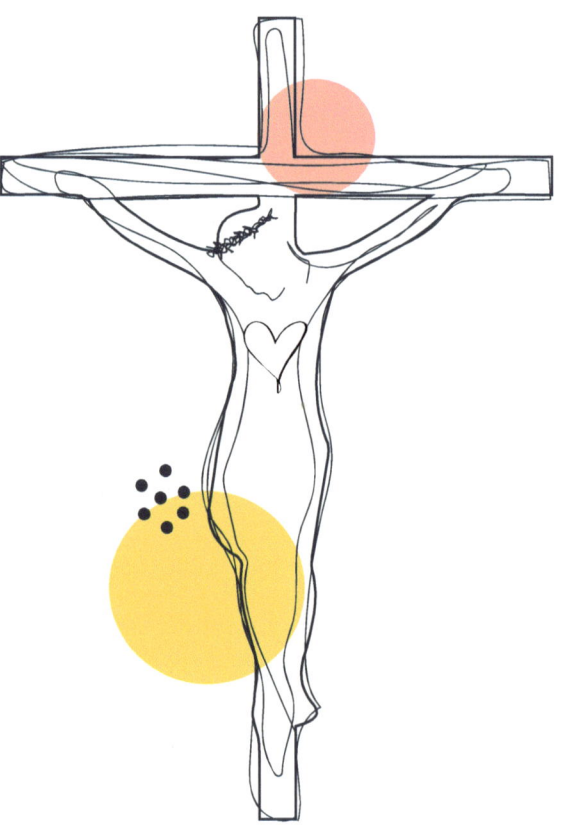

The Journey

With each new day comes the gift of hope and another chance to experience something amazing. It is futile to waste it on past regrets or worries about the future. Be present in this moment and the good things that it brings.

Return

Far, far from the peaceful shores of home
My desperate heart did roam
Looking for my so-called freedom yall
Avoiding my predestined kingdom call
Searching for love and prosperity
All caught up in myself, I had no charity
I was living high on the world
Dressed in diamonds and pearls
Just chillin' with my home girls
Running away from responsibility
Hiding from all accountability
Ducking and dodging authority
Looked up one day lost in insanity
Sin had its hold on me, I could not break free
My so-called friends were nowhere to be
Spent all my inheritance down to the last dime
Rent was past due and I was running out of time
Living a bootlegged life in the gutter of my soul
Out here in a world filled with hatred, so dark and cold

I can't make it out here on my own
And just like the prodigal son, I said...
I think I'll go back home
And the song writer wrote
Take me back, take me back dear Lord
to the place where I first received You
Take me back, take me back dear Lord where I first believed

Return, Return to Jesus while breath still remains
And the blood is still running warm through your veins
Return, Return to Jesus He's waiting for you
With outstretched hands and life brand new
His forgiveness is truly everlasting
His love withstands raging seas and stormy weather
And His mercy – Oh His mercy endureth forever
Return to the fellowship, the family, the fold
And like the prodigal son I said
I think I'll go back home

Hope

With each new day comes the gift of hope
and another chance to experience something amazing
It is futile to waste it on past regrets
or worries about the future
Be present in this moment
and the lessons that it brings
One may say, there is nothing good about today –
troubles are all I see
But imagine that it's true –
that you'll find just what you're looking for
So why not look with Great Expectations
as you face each day
God's promises are based on "will be done"
not "might be done," not "maybe"
And if a detour should detain you along life's journey
follow the Light back to the highway of hope
Find your way back.

Another Monday

As I laid unconscious
To the world around me
Carelessly I slumbered and slept
Awakened by the warm sun
Against my timeless face
Without hoping - Without a prayer
But trusting that he
Would come for me
Faithfully, he returned
Bearing the gift of yet
Another sunrise
Another misty breeze
Another taste of wheat bread and honey
Another Monday

A Tribute to Single Mothers

She may be divorced, widowed or unwed
But we encourage her to lift up her head
For God loves mothers and not just some
There is a special place in His heart for the single mom
Looking down at her swollen belly big and round
Heart broken into pieces shattered on the ground
Passers-by they point, whisper and stare
Casting their judgment without a care
But God knows all of her hopes and dreams
And He sees her tears flowing like streams
Bills are always plenty yet friends are sometimes few
But know that God will always see you through
Like a tree that's planted by the waters, she shall not be moved
She ain't going nowhere. She'll be right there my baby sweet
Praising God for milk and enough food to eat
For baby clothes on your back and little shoes on your feet
Watching your every breathe – your every heart beat

She may be divorced, widowed or unwed
Adoption, abandoned, aborted – No! She chose you instead
She chose love with so little to gain
She chose love in spite of her pain
Now I lay me down to sleep, and lonely I weep, weep, weep
Never quite reaching that deep, deep, sleep
Nights spent dreaming while angels watched over her baby's bed
Yet angry devils danced through her head
They say you'll never make it on your own
They say that you'll always be alone
Suddenly awakened by a gentle sigh,
a midnight cry in the darkness
Hush now baby, mama's here
Daddy is gone but I will always be near
Hush now baby, stop your fuss
Jesus will take good care of us.
Jesus loves the little children, all the children or the world
Red and yellow, black and white, they are precious in His sight
Jesus loves the little children of the world
And by the grace of our Lord who suffered and bled
We can trust in God to do just what He said
And give Him all of the glory for the victories ahead

It's Later Than You Think

Time is on my heels like a sprinter's wind
Shadows chase the light as the sun descends
Awakened by God not just by instinct
He said wake up child, it's later than you think
Time is running out for the truth to be told
To give someone a word that may save their soul
The night is nigh – day passeth in a blink
Better get up child, it's later than you think

No One Like Me

I spent my youth in search of me
Didn't know who I was supposed to be
Chameleon-like creature, changing shape
Changing color, a mere reflection
Moving about without direction
Invisibly undercover
Just hoping to be discovered
Like a child playing hide-and-seek by myself
There was no one to find me
Then one day
I heard the voice of Jesus say
Tag, I found you. And now you're it
Touch somebody
Discover the undiscoverable
Love the unlovable
See the invisible
Hear the unheard
Achieve the impossible
Break down old walls
Enter that open door
Experiencing God like never before
It's okay to feel what you feel
But speak truth to yourself
And just be real

The Mentor

See a young misguided girl
Looking out across a grown up world
Too confused to sleep, nights spent tossing and turning
Acting out in school, hindering her learning
Standing in need of a mentor and friend
Someone to teach her how to play again
Bow down and teach her how to pray again

We can't make it out here on our own
God did not design us to go it alone
Not only do we need God and God's Word, but we need God's people
A people inspired with a passion for Christ and others
We need teachers, leaders, sisters, aunts and we need mothers
To lift up our heads in times of despair and desperation
Shining bright that radiant light of hope and inspiration

Mentors have a great work to do
Someone that understands what we're going thru
From our youth all the way into womanhood
We remain in need of a strong sisterhood

You see, God could have left me at the place where I fell
Standing before Him like the woman at the well
Now wrapped in His love – confessed and forgiven –
Washed in His blood, now victoriously I have risen!
Up from the place where I used to be
Hand in hand with a mentor who cares for me
Helping me to become the best me that I can be
Seeing past my false pretense and external blunders
To a source of emotions torn asunder
My God is a Wonder!
For He sent me a mentor, imperfect yet kind
Able to uplift this old heart of mine
Yes we have risen!
Up from the place where we used to be
Hand in hand united and free!

Restlessness

What is this that I'm feeling - It's hard to describe
Strain and struggle and sadness – a restlessness inside
Hopeless - useless – pointless – life that has no meaning
An insignificant existence - a worthless state of being
Lonely days are many – but there are people everywhere
Tugging me in every direction – far more than I can bear

Children they need raising – can't get them to stop crying
Parents they keep aging – can't get them to stop dying
Relationships are stressful – I think I'll just... stop trying
Why do my friends forsake me? Acquaintances come and go
But when they need something from me - they come a calling tho

The days, the weeks, the months, the years - my youth is almost spent
Like that last ten dollars in my pocket - I can't tell you where it went
This restlessness overwhelms me - It starts with negative thoughts
And snowballs down a steep hill - to a place where depression is wrought
Maxed out – menopausal mess – that's who I've come to be
The more I try to live right, problems are all I see

I bowed down on my knees to pray
But didn't know what to say
So much disappointment in my heart
I didn't know where to start
Have you ever found yourself without a prayer somehow?
Mighty prayer warrior – where is your prayer now?

With the help of the Lord I managed to make it here
Where I found sisters just like me tenderly standing near
Then the Holy Spirit took hold of all my mercy me's and moans
And He heard my despairing cries and He pitied every grown

Someone said, just hold on to God's unchanging hand
Someone told me don't give up – He'll rescue you again
They said, everything will be all right – all is not lost
He knows your every weakness – and He already paid the cost
God gave us ministries to keep us close together
By loving one another we can battle any weather
Life is full of difficulties – great trouble across the land
Yet it is on the promises of God on which we can stand

So do not fear, for I am with you; (says the Lord)
do not be dismayed, for I am your God.
I will strengthen you and help you;
I will uphold you with my righteous right hand.
My grace is sufficient for thee:
for my strength is made perfect in weakness.
Come to Me, all you who labor and are heavy laden, and I will give you rest.
And the peace of God, which transcends all understanding,
will guard your hearts and your minds in Christ Jesus.
Isa. 41.10, Cor. 12:9, Matt. 11:28, Phil. 4:7

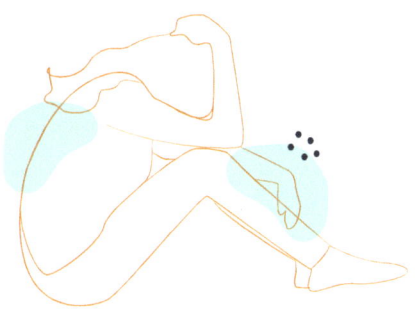

Snowflake

When I was a girl
I dreamed of a world
Of beautiful people
Unique as snowflakes
Floating on the wind
Coming together as friends
To cover the earth
With sheets of pure white
From city roof tops
To the mountain peaks
On boundless plains
As far as the eye can see
Now the girl
in a polluted world
Cold as a snowman
Melting in the light
As her season ends
A new Spring begins
The snowflake no longer
Yet a shapeless puddle
Evaporating in the air
Ascending from the Earth
Back into the heavens
From whence she came

Heart & Soul

Create in me a clean heart, oh God;
and renew a right spirit within me.
Psalm 51:10

Burst Free

It seems impossible to control
Matters of the heart and soul

To subdue the tears of joy and pain
Is like trying to halt the rain

So allow yourself a hardy cry
Exceed that simple sigh

Resist temptation to be too proud
To lean back and laugh out loud

Take courage to examine every part
For a deep cleansing of the heart

Set free the stories that lie untold
Ignite a flame that stirs the soul

A heart hidden from the world
A long-awaited pebble to pearl

A soulful song unsung
Til breath-filled lungs
Burst free!

Peace Offering

Of all the gifts in the world –
Riches and wealth, silver and gold
Fortune and fame, mansions and Mercedes
Amazing abilities, wondrous adventures
Talents, skills, knowledge and education
Beauty and romance
Strength, endurance, speed and agility
So many gifts, so many, many gifts
And just when I thought that I had none ...
Tilting upward toward the heavens
I stood pondering my very worth
Then the quiet voice of peace
Rushed over me like cooling waters
In the heat of a summer day
Inhaling the joy of love and life
Exhaling all doubt that I am gifted
God could have given me many things
But He chose to give me the gift of peace
Sleep comes easy and joy comes in the morn
sweet dreams... good night...

My Perfect Day

Sitting in a vineyard on a perfect day
In a beautiful linen dress flowing when I sway
The warm sun against my skin, a gentle breeze
Dancing in my hair and whisking thru the trees
A tender kiss upon my face
As Don and I toast and embrace
He stands to say a prayer of thanksgiving
For all the family still among the living
And for those watching from the heavens above
In a vineyard just like this smiling down with love
Chris laughing out loud fills my heart with glee
Kisha with stylus and digital canvas sits close to me
Painting the children, grandchildren and great grands too
Playing in the meadow and doing what children do
Stringed instruments play a song that fills the air
A peaceful melody from a place – don't know where
Butterflies appear and dance overhead
Hungry strangers sit at our table gladly fed
Maya Angelou in deep recitation just happens by
We share a poem together over coffee and apple pie
As I take a bite I sigh, Mmmmm God is so good!
Gave me the desires of my heart, just like he said he would
Then Jesus appears and tells a funny joke
And we all just laugh out loud with nothing more say
Oh but what... a perfect day

Dusty Gray

Whether it's black-on-black, white-on-black, yellow, red or brown crime...
Mental struggles strike without prejudice in the minds of those who have no hope
And sorrow has no preference of color, age, status, school, zip code, or faith

Hatred blindly sets its aim on innocent lives
who dare to exist in its reckless path
There our children fall, suffer and die and they all bleed red.

So let us cry out for them all, whether it is a white school in Florida
or a black neighborhood on the windy streets of Chicago
A crowd of young people celebrating life at a concert
Or one innocent black boy walking home from the store

Let us cry out for them all
Echoing into the darkness
A mother's heavy wailing and
A father's howling rage
Yes, it all hurts the same
When will we understand
The message is clear
Hatred and sin are the enemies here
At war with all mankind
And if the gift of life cannot unite us
Then we'll find equality in the grave
When our skins all turn a dusty gray

Warm Towels

Grabbed up a bunch of hot towels
Fluffy and fresh from the dryer
Nabbed them all up tightly
Not one left behind in the spin
Hugged safely in my arms
Careful to not drop even one
Tossed them on the sofa
So I could snuggle in the pile
Like a warm embrace
Like a new baby's smile
Who knew
Folding warm towels
Could be sweet serenity
To a retiree - an escapee
Set free from the workplace
Now folding warm towels
While listening to my jams
Still clothed in my jams
Slow down - not too fast now
Want this moment to last now
Til the warmness cools
Or I fall fast deep asleep
While folding these soft, clean
... warm towels

Weary Feet

Walking, running
Weary feet
Sat to release
A load of heaviness
Stripped
Naked feet
Lowered down
In the refreshing
Warm blue water
Finger tips
A touch
Soft like Kindness
Willingly washing
Unworthy weary feet
Humbly receiving
This strange love

John 13:1-17

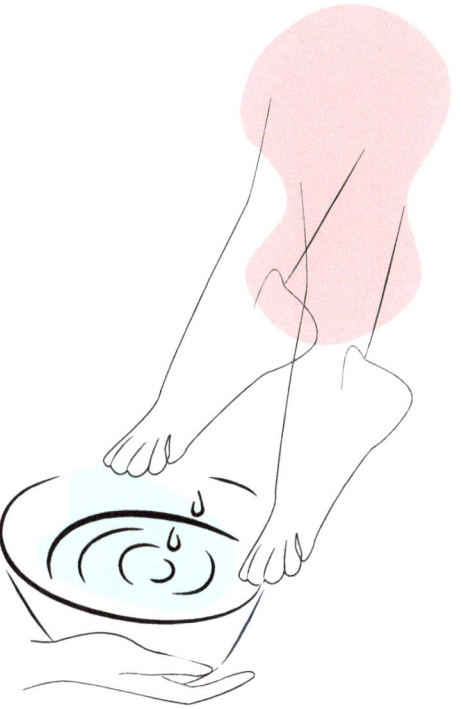

The Passion

Jesus became who we are ...
So that we could become who He is
... That's love

Hard to Love

I could tell she wanted to touch him
But even more she wanted to be touched
She sat half turned in her chair next to him
and waited for him to gesture toward her
He sat with arms crossed as he sternly
stared forward into space
Yet he saw nothing but her
I could tell that he was blinded by desire
Yet he continued to look away
She looked at him
then slowly touched her head
to his shoulder
He remained paralyzed by pride
his ego commanded his heart to hide
His arms stretched up over his head
It was an obvious fight
And yet I knew then
That passion would win

She moved her head away
and again she waited
His stubbornness was strong
But not for long
Uncontrollably she fingered his hair
grooming him tenderly
like a mother's care
Then his arm moved gently
across her back
and the inevitable embrace
finally happened as her head
rested softly in his arms

Why is it so hard to feel
To respond and just be real
Why so slow to connect
Yet so quick to reject

Why is it so hard to love?

The Totality of Love

What could be more romantic than being with you
Sipping Champaign under the lights of a city view
As we listen to our favorite jazzmic songs
Fine wine and roses until the break of dawn
You frisk my mind with gentle conversation
Filling me with a tantalizing sensation
That sweeps me totally off my feet

Gift shops and coffee as we waltz through town
Night spots still open and gettin' down
Tightly clutched hand in hand our warmth flows
A tender kiss shared between us and love grows

Is this the totality of love?

Words that settle cool like morning dew
Passionately echoing "baby I love you"
Longing for you and begging you to stay
Yearning and missing you when you're away
Don't need no symbolic red roses
No heart shapes and passionate poses
Is this the totality of love?

Did I mention the hurt, did I mention the pain
The driving me crazy and hopelessly insane
Got me walking around in the rain!
Broken hearted – emotions guarded
Is this the totality of love?

...no

"Love is patient, love is kind. It does not envy, it does not boast, it is not
proud. It is not rude, it is not self-seeking, it is not easily angered, it keeps
no record of wrongs. Love does not delight in evil but rejoices with the truth.
It always protects, always trusts, always hopes, always perseveres. Love never
fails." I Corinthians 13:-6-8

Now that's the totality of love

Give Love a Chance

There love sits alone
In the waiting room
Of the hearts of man
Patiently anticipating
Its next encounter
Receive me now
Don't turn me away
Not this time
If I appear undesirable
If I stumble and stutter
Or my words all run together
Don't leave me...
Don't turn away...
Stay

Black Orchestra

Play for me
With your strings
Your horns
Your pounding drums
Stir up in me
Emotions numbed
Buried deep within
Awaken old passions
Make them anew
Set me free
Black Orchestra
Play for me

Tones of Splendor

Mellow alto tones of splendor
So smooth and laid back
Burn till my heart surrenders

And the sun turns to black

Rhythm strumming my spine
With magical fingers of gold
Calm this old soul of mine
That it may never grow too old

Music floating on a cool summer breeze
Sends me dancing under strobing lights
Touching me with a tease
Taking my soul to higher heights

Such mellow tones of splendor
My naked heart you do reveal
Emotions free and sweetly tender
Is just the way I like to feel

Right Now

If I only had a bit of their energy
Where does it all come from?
Pure, raw, fearless energy
Ready to soar and take on the world
It's not so much about what they have
But more about what they do not have
They are as light as feathers
Floating freely on the wind
Weightless containers
Ready to be filled to the brim
with the newness of now
Not yesterday's useless baggage
Nor hope of treasures for tomorrow

Free of dusty old dreams
And lusty longings
Those rusty old ruts are a bore
It's "right now"
that burns to the core
And makes them yearn for more
The present is enough
Right now is all they need
Each moment is a present
Not one gift goes unwrapped
Big boxes of happiness
Small packages of joy
Hugs, kisses and hopeful wishes
One by one they unwrap them all

Hard Enough

Am I trying hard enough
Am I doing my best
To reach beyond man's accolades
To do more than pass the test
What is more fulfilling
What grander feats there lie
Than the measure of mere men
Who dare to touch the sky

The Dreamer

Your young men will see visions,
your old men will dream dreams.

Acts 2:17

A Dream Come True

Night dreams occur in an unconscious state of mind
when a series of thoughts, images, sensations and emotions
flood your mind without intent
Many times night dreams will slip back
into the deep subconscious
too far away to recall

However, daydreams are intentional
and may linger for a life-time
Like that so-called dream job
business venture or that perfect mate
However, there are some bright ideas
that were never meant to replace true purpose
And then there are those who are destined for
a dream come true.

As a dreamer, I dream of a place
that I can call my own
Its welcoming doors opening wide
to engulf the customer
like a warm embrace

The smell of fresh coffee
and danishes fill the room
saturating the senses
and teasing the taste buds
like a French kiss
Before your next step
your eyes would gaze
upon a captivating canvas of art
Body swaying to soothing music
The beat tickles your toes to tap
I dream of a place
filled with inspiration
encouragement, education, awareness
laughter, compassion, loveliness
cleanliness, rest, peace and friendship –
A safe place for creative Christian expression
Where sweet visions come to life!

Mama?

Mama, what did you dream of?
What were your hopes
and the desires of your heart?
Did you ever sit daydreaming?
Wishing upon a star
Did being the best mama
Adequately satisfy
Surely you wanted something
That was just for you
Did you want to ...

>   dance like a princess
>   sing like an angel
>   see the world
>   sail upon the sea
>   make grand speeches
>   drive a race car
>   climb a mountain ...

Mama, what did you dream of?
Someday sitting in heaven's garden
we'll talk all about it

I believe my children know
The things I daydream of
And when I'm gone from this world
They will have known my heart

My Africa

Sweet shades of blackness in a land golden and green
Mighty rivers flowing toward waterfalls cool and clean
Vast plains spread far and wide
Wild animals in full stride
Like the heart of a peoples' pride
Running free ... Just as God created me to be
Sleeping little babies safe at rest
Tightly bundled beneath their mama's breasts
And the day is done
As the evening sun
Descends into the horizon
My Africa – Let us celebrate freedom
In all its magnificence and splendor!

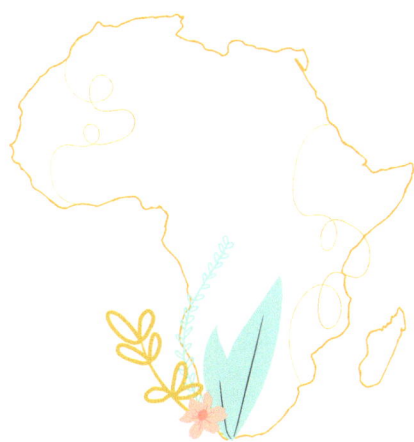

Faces

In the late hours of the night
Flickering through the trees
I see a fluorescent light
As the noise ends quietness begins
The mood changes and once again
Loneliness is set free
In my head familiar faces I see
Of loved ones gone on before me
The way she used to laugh and smile
Made me glad for awhile
Yet then I saw the tears she shed
Her many faces dancing in my head
I can almost see her standing before me
Risen from the grave
Like a lonely soul lost at sea
Among the restless waves
Words unspoken, an irreversible time
Jesters, good deeds, thoughts trapped in my mind
Wishes that will never come true
Clear reflections of a face I once knew
Dedicated to my sisters Mattie, Linda and Brenda.
May they rest in peace

The Night

In the stillness of the night
The gentle swaying of palm leaves
And the ocean's waters rippling in the wind
Change the mood like the colors of the sky
Mightier than a ship's steadfast anchor
Gripped firmly to the bottom of the sea
Yet by some unseen, mysterious power
The forces of the night are once again set free
In the late hours of the night
Glistening through the trees
I see the light
As blaring sounds subside quietness tips in
And timid spirits take to the wind
Against the darkness of the night
A full moon and a starlit sky
Paint the heavens without borders
Like a picture without a frame
There is magic in the night
And the dusk and dawning hours
This day forever lost in twilight
Never to return

The Chestnut Stallion

As I stood there in a daze
Quite unconcerned with the world
Thinking of golden fields of wheat
Wildflowers a bloom
in colors of purple and pink
And thinking of a certain horse
Whose coat was chestnut brown
all shiny and smooth
What a handsome stallion he was
There I sat atop his warm back
The sun shining against us
As we sored across an open field
Chasing anxiously for tomorrow
Leaving the day's trouble far behind
Strength, beauty and freedom
A new identity not my own
With the grace of a dancer
And the speed of light
We sored through space and time
Then my consciousness awakened
With a loud roar
As the bus approached the stop
The doors swung open
I climbed aboard
And the doors...
Closed tightly behind me

A Place Beyond

There must be a place
Invisible to those of this life
There must truly be a place
For I have seen the face of death
And as death came upon her
Like a mighty eagle
Swooping down upon its prey
She became changed
In her eyes I could see
That she was no longer with me
But in a place beyond my sight
Beyond my comprehension
Beyond my grasp
As I did reach out for her

Her voice so weak
Now clear and loud
Spoke to loved ones
Long passed on before her
Images reflected in her eyes
As she looked upon their faces
And in that brief encounter
Joy, happiness, relief and sadness
Rushed in like a gust of wind
Then vanished in an instant
There is such a place
Right here in this space
For she was beside me, yet far away
I truly believe that loved ones
Are reunited in death
In a place beyond

Distance Between Us

Distant lands far from home
In search of you my heart did roam
Natural beauty and cultural song
As I think of you all the day long
Artistic sculpture and remnants of old
Canvasses of emotions framed in gold
Painted in colors that bring them to life
Pictures of happiness, joy, misery and strife
Impressions of life long ago spent
Memorial gifts from heaven sent
A special character all your own
This land I could have known
Distant friend, whom I should have met
Oceans and mountains between us, and yet
Though much too far from here to see
I feel your soul in search of me

A Window View

I, on one side of the glass
Stand looking through the window
Of my glassy eyes
As you walk through the mirror
And step softly on the other side
The other side of my window
As I wipe away the moist fog of breath
The view becomes clearer
Almost real enough to touch
The muffled sounds of festival
And cordial conversations
Clearly heard but misunderstood
As the words seem to flow
Like the ruffling tail of a kite
Across a clear blue sky
Farewell my distant one
As you walk through my window.
View the world through the eyes
Of an old romantic like me
Reaching out for your fantasy
While clinching tightly to reality
The reality of life is Love

Prince in a Dream Land

Once upon a time in a land unseen and a time untold
There lived a handsome prince mighty and bold
His hair was as dark as a moonless night
Yet his hazel eyes glistened like the stars so bright
He floated two inches from the ground
And could speak to every living creature around
Haughtily he glided over the plains so green
Purifying the water and keeping the air clean
Every day was a festival of music and feast
Celebrating the victory of the slaying of the beast
The beast of evil, darkness and fear
Who brought nothing but death and sadness here
They came from miles and miles around
To see this dream land others had found
Rainbows and cherry blossoms in bloom
Blue birds flying and singing an enchanted tune
Although it was day and the sun was shining high
There were stars like magic twinkling in the sky
And tear drops like stars came falling from his eye
As all stood in amazement to see their prince cry
The prince, a bit sad, yet proud and grand
Had everything he wanted except that special woman
But where could one find a woman as grand as he
To live beneath this rainbow until eternity
They adorned their daughters with satin and pearls
Heads filled with orchids, and daisies and curls
Precious silks, priceless stones, laces and such
But after all was done his heart was untouched
...only in my dreams

The Victories

Rise up and shine for your light has come.

Isa. 60:1

The Victorious Woman

Before the glorious sunrise the victorious woman awakens
With the promise that the righteous will never be forsaken
Reshaped and molded by God's chastening hand
Like the woman at the well before her Lord she stands
Born into sin, now confessed and forgiven
Wrapped in His love, now victoriously she is risen!
She is not your average soap opera queen
But a woman with active passions and dreams
Of building up the Kingdom, lifting up His name
And spreading the gospel for she is not ashamed
Filled with His power, not fear – she's not weak
Nor is she timid, she knows when to speak
Integrity is her high ground. Humility is her strength
Faith is her stronghold, for her help is heaven sent
She manages her home, business and all aspects of her life
She does not try to be the husband; she knows that she's the wife
She is kind, gentle, modest and loving toward the poor

Graciously she gives her little and the Lord gives her more
She does not eat the bread of idleness
Her children rise up and call her blessed
Her husband – Oh how he praises her
Giving thanks to God in his every prayer
For her incorruptible beauty that is hidden in her heart
Not pretentiously and outwardly just trying to look the part
Her fear of the Lord gives her wisdom –
faithful instruction is on her tongue
She cares for the old and counsels with the young
She sings a song that no song bird has ever sang
And all through the house the praises of God rang
Once battered and bound by the world – imprisoned
Washed in His blood, now victoriously she is risen
Stand now risen with the Crucified Savior who lives
For these and other virtues to all He freely gives

The Dedication of Life

To the earth's entire population
Whatever your race, creed, color or occupation
I send you this letter of notification
Informing you of your current situation

It has been my personal observation
Through a brief and informal investigation
That we are headed for a destination
Of death, destruction and endless damnation

A deadly disease is in circulation
HIV, AIDS and the COVID persuasion
Spreading the globe from nation to nation
Murder and hate-filled acts of abomination
Loveless, adulterous, lustful fornication
Unbelievable sites beyond the imagination

I must confess my admiration
For those of faithful dedication
Spreading righteous communication
Without shame or humiliation

Standing up with pride and conviction
Against drug and alcohol addiction
By stating fact and not fiction

While many worry about inflation
Others endure hunger and starvation
Some die from food contamination
It's just a pitiful situation!

So who in this world knows the solution
To child pornography and prostitution
Doesn't anybody have a resolution
To change the destiny of our institution

I extend to you this cordial invitation
To join in worldwide participation
Promoting peace, hope and inspiration
To each and every generation

We all need hope – we need restoration
A Savior to free us from our desperation
His name is Jesus - God's dedication
Who sacrificed His life for our salvation

Power Break

Sipping my vanilla latte
At my little desk by the window
Working under fluorescent lights
As I look out at a misty day
A day that the Lord has made
I ponder how He is a Wonder
I anticipate great things
Even in my incompleteness
Because I know
That He will finish
His good work in me
I cannot find regret
Nor disappointment
Because He has hid it from me
I see only His power
And what He can do
Even in me

Black Cotton

I was born on the other
side of the tracks
With nappy hair and
skin jet black
When popular was pretty
and pretty was bright
Which is what you were called
if your skin was light
Fine baby hair
framing the face
Softly lain
like amber lace
Not Jheri curls
natural twirling swirls
Gratefully now I see
the beauty that's in me
God didn't slip
I was chocolate dipped
A face not easily forgotten
dark sun-kissed skin
nestled in black cotton

Thankful

All of my life – God has been good to me
In the midst of loss and the joys of new birth
There have been struggles and hardship
and showers of blessings
Through sickness and in health
Through ups and downs
From poverty to plenty
I thank Him for it all!

If I had 10,000 tongues

I'd tell of God's many miracles on earth
And his mysteries throughout the Universe
I would speak of all his wondrous acts
Not fairytales – but biblical facts
I would thank him for each and every one
Yet and still I'd never be done

If I had 10,000 tongues

I'd thank him for the struggles in life
They've made me strong in this fight
When standing at decisions gate
I thank him for the stop, the go, the not yet... wait
I thank the Lord for the freedom to run
From the rising of the dawn
To the setting of the sun

If I had 10,000 tongues

I would call each blessing out by name
And with every breath I'd proclaim
It was by God's power that mountains rose up
And streams do flow and volcanoes erupt
And praising blue birds sing worship songs
Yes, and I would gratefully echo along

If I had 10,000 tongues

For food and shelter from the stormy weather
As winds of destruction passed me by
And his brilliant light opened up the sky
Though deadly decease crept near my door
Health and hope was again restored
For he stained the doorpost of my heart
With the blood of the Lamb reaching every part

If I had 10,000 tongues

For your kindness, forgiveness, your mercy, your grace
For your faithfulness along this race
I'd thank you for every blessing and name each one
Yet and still I'd never be done

If I had 10,000 tongues

Black Lives Matter

Like all of creation
MIRACULOUSLY
God made me.
CAREFULLY
He placed my inward parts.
SPECIFICALLY
He gifted me. He set me apart
as if I were
PARTICULARLY
special in his heart.
UNIQUELY
He imprinted my fingers.
INDIVIDUALLY
He curled each strand.
METICULOUSLY
He shaped my face THEN...
INTENTIONALLY
He – colored – me – BLACK

Grateful

Some were created to do big things
Some made just to enjoy them
Some were created with great beauty
Some gifted to create it
Some exist to be peacemakers
Some just to live peaceful
Some find deep love in life
Some give it all away
Some have wings of an eagle flying high
Bright streaking light across the sky
Some have the wings of a butterfly
A glimpse of freedom fluttering by
Some bring tides of joy
Some rejoice where there is no joy
Some were born to be great
Some just to be grateful
Oh and I am grateful

www.ingramcontent.com/pod-product-compliance
Lightning Source LLC
Chambersburg PA
CBHW040857120626
46551CB00001B/59